102 ESL G
New and Prospective Teachers

By Miles Jaworski

Copyright © Miles Jaworski 2013
The author asserts the moral right to be identified as the author of this work.
All rights reserved. No part of this book may be reproduced or transmitted in any form or by any means, electronic, mechanical, photocopying or otherwise, without the prior written permission of the author.

Other books by this author

<u>102 ESL Games and Activities for Kids</u>

<u>Basic English Grammar: A Guide for New and Prospective ESL Teachers</u>

<u>English Grammar Exercises: A Complete Guide to English Tenses for ESL Students</u>

Table of contents

0. Introduction
1. A Valentine's story (Past simple)
2. Halloween stories (Past simple etc.)
3. Did you use to? (Used to / Past simple)
4. Why did you write? (Past simple)
5. Police and Thieves (Past simple)
6. The last time (Past simple)
7. A story in your pocket (Past simple / Past continuous / Past perfect)
8. Verb challenge (Verb forms)
9. Irregular verbs bingo (Past tense irregular verbs)
10. Past participle pelmanism (Past participle verb forms)
11. Are you experienced? (Present perfect / Past simple)
12. Hotter hotter…(Present perfect)
13. My perfect life (Present perfect simple / Present perfect continuous)
14. Find a classmate who (Present simple)
15. Frequency predictions (Present simple / Adverbs and expressions of frequency)
16. A question of habit (Present simple / Adverbs of frequency)
17. Who is it? (Present simple / Describing people)
18. Carrot (question forms)
19. Ask me anything (Question forms)
20. Give me a question (Question forms)
21. Sausages (Question forms)
22. Dead or alive (Question forms)
23. Who am I? (Yes / No questions in various tenses)
24. What do you do? (Jobs vocabulary / Question forms)
25. The extraordinarily long sentence (Sentence formation)
26. Three in a row (Sentence formation)

27. Sentence jumble (Sentence formation)
28. What am I doing? (Present continuous)
29. How am I doing it? (Present continuous / Adverbs of action)
30. Small talk (Various / Fluency skills)
31. Quick debates (Various / Fluency skills)
32. Survival situation (Various / Fluency skills)
33. Dice talking (Various / Fluency skills)
34. Experts (Various / Fluency skills)
35. Don't stop talking (Various / Fluency skills)
36. The goat, the tiger and the cabbage (Various / Fluency skills)
37. Find out about me (Various / Fluency skills)
38. What do we have in common? (Various / Fluency skills)
39. Student line up (Various / Fluency skills)
40. The seven wonders
41. The truth or a dirty lie? (Various / Fluency skills)
42. Classroom theater (Various)
43. Odd one out (Vocabulary)
44. Vocabulary swap (Vocabulary)
45. What am I drawing? (Vocabulary)
46. Vocabulary race (Vocabulary)
47. Word association (Vocabulary)
48. What does it mean? (Vocabulary)
49. Topics (Vocabulary)
50. ABC topics (Vocabulary)
51. Chain spelling (Vocabulary / Spelling)
52. Constantinople (Vocabulary / Spelling)
53. Anagrams (Vocabulary / Spelling)
54. Donkey (Vocabulary / Spelling)
55. What's in the bag? (Vocabulary / Spelling)
56. Extremely long words (Vocabulary / Spelling)
57. Clap spelling (Spelling)
58. Crosswords construction (Vocabulary / Definitions /

Synonyms / Antonyms)
59. Hot seat (Vocabulary / Definitions / Synonyms / Antonyms)
60. Password (Vocabulary / Definitions / Synonyms / Antonyms)
61. Password prohibition (Vocabulary / Definitions / Synonyms / Antonyms)
62. Definition bluff (Vocabulary / Definitions / Synonyms / Antonyms)
63. Sentence song (Vocabulary / Listening skills)
64. Tape-recorder dictation (Listening skills)
65. Whispered sentences (Listening skills)
66. Aliens (Language of description / relative clauses)
67. Shouting Dictation (Listening skills / Reading skills)
68. Running Dictation (Listening skills / Reading skills)
69. Proverb match (Listening skills / Reading skills / Proverbs)
70. Student story order (Reading skills / listening skills)
71. Looking for love (Reading skills / Writing skills)
72. Superlative students (Superlative adjectives)
73. Comparative students (Comparative adjectives)
74. Love or money (Comparative adjectives)
75. Blindfolded directions (Directions / Imperatives)
76. Map reading (Directions / Imperatives)
77. Animal clock (Telling the time)
78. Clock race (Telling the time)
79. My beautiful living room (Prepositions of place / Furniture)
80. It's my life (Various)
81. Articles shout out (Articles)
82. Cheater! (Cardinal numbers / Plurals)
83. Bing bong bang (Cardinal numbers)
84. Ordinal bing bong bang (Ordinal numbers)
85. Compound word quiz (Compound words)
86. What did you buy? (Expressions of quantity)

87. Thank you so much! (Polite requests)
88. Tongue twister demo (Pronunciation)
89. General knowledge quiz (Various)
90. Partial pictures (Modal verbs / Adverbs of possibility and probability)
91. Four in a row tenses (Tenses)
92. Tornado (Various)
93. Half conditionals (Conditional tenses)
94. Animal antics (2nd conditional)
95. If this person were… (2nd conditional)
96. Grammars swat (Various)
97. Problems, problems (Advice)
98. Name ball (Names)
99. Listen to me! (Language to show interest)
100. Map race (Countries / Nationalities / People)
101. A good sentence? (Various / Error correction)
102. Word sprint (Sentence structure)

Introduction

A lively, dynamic atmosphere is essential in the ESL classroom; one where students feel motivated to communicate in English but are unafraid of making mistakes. Communicative, engaging ESL games and activities are an excellent way of promoting this atmosphere and should, of course, be incorporated into most lessons.

Within this book, you will find games and activities that can be used as warmers, coolers or fillers, for example, The Very Long Sentence or Carrot; games and activities that practice or introduce specific language points, for example, Police and Thieves or Clock Race; and games and activities that focus on improving fluency, for example, Dice Talking or Survival Situation.

It is almost always better, when possible, to choose one or more of your more advanced students to help you demonstrate any game or activity, rather than simply trusting that any explanation you give is understood. That way lies confusion and frustration!

In addition, with all activities, you, the teacher, should be circulating as the students are working in order to provide assistance and to note down examples of both good and bad language. You are thus able to offer feedback on the students' performances once the activity or game is over.

I have provided approximate timings for all the activities and games, but that's what they are: approximate timings. Each class is different so do not tie yourself to these.

What I would advise though, is always stopping an activity before the students get bored. This way they will remain engaged throughout the activity, and you may be able to use the activity once more with the same class.

Enjoy your lessons!

1. A Valentine's story

Language / Skill practiced: Past simple
Time: 30 mins
Language level: Elementary to intermediate

Arrange the class, on chairs, into a circle and give each student a sheet of paper. Explain to the class that they are going to write a love or Valentine's story and that they must write full sentence answers to your questions. Ask your first question, "What was his name?" Each student writes the answer at the top of her piece of paper and then folds the paper back so that the sentence is hidden. They then pass their piece of paper to the student on their left and answer your next question, "What was her name?" before folding back the paper once more and again passing it to the person on their left. Continue in this way for about ten questions, asking questions such as, "What did he say to her?" "Where did they go?" "Where did they have their first kiss?" etc. When you have finished asking questions, ask the students to read their stories and, if you choose, correct any errors.

2. Halloween stories

Language / Skill practiced: Past simple / Past continuous/ Past perfect
Time: 20 to 25 mins
Language level: Elementary to intermediate

Write the following sentence on the board: "It was a dark, moonless night and I was walking home alone when I heard a strange noise."

Arrange the class into a circle and invite the students in turn to add between one and three sentences to the story. For example:

S1: The noise was like a growl and I started to walk faster.
S2: And I could hear footsteps behind me.
S3: So I started to walk even faster and I heard the growl again. I was so scared and started to run, but then I tripped over.
S4: My leg was broken and I…..

And so on.

Continue for several rounds so that each student has a chance to speak two or three times. Then place the students into groups to repeat the activity with a new first scary sentence.

3. Did you use to?

Language / Skill practiced: Used to / Past simple
Time: 15 mins
Language level: Pre-intermediate

Ask the class to stand up. Give each student a slip of paper on which you have typed a topic such as "favorite food," "get up," "sports like," "favorite movie," and "games play" etc. Students find a partner and ask two questions based on the prompt on their slip of paper; one question in the present simple, and one using "used to." For example:

S1 (slip says games / play): What games do you like to play?
S2: Grand theft auto on the x box.
S1: Oh, Ok. And what games did you use to like when you were 5 yrs old?
S2: I used to like hide and seek!

When both students have asked and answered their questions they swap their slips of paper so they have a new prompt and find a new partner. After 10 minutes, stop the activity and put the students in groups of three to tell their group what they found out about their classmates.

4. Why did you write …?

Language / Skill practiced: Past simple
Time: 15 mins
Language level: Elementary to pre-intermediate

Ask students to write down 4 past dates that are important to them. For example, "16th Feb 1999," "1978," "last Friday" and "2005." Put students in pairs to swap pieces of paper and ask and answer the question, "Why did you write date?" Students should answer in full sentences. For example:

S1: Why did you write 1978?
S2: Because I was born in 1978. Why did you write 16th

Feb 1999?
S1: Because that was when I got married

And so on.

5. Police and thieves

Language / Skill practiced: Past simple
Time: 15 mins
Language level: Elementary to pre-intermediate

You will almost certainly need to pre-teach the words, "suspect" and "alibi" before you begin this activity. Tell the class that there has been a robbery at the school between 7 pm and 11:00 pm and that the police suspect two people. The police think that the two suspects did the crime together, but that the suspects claim that at 7:00pm they were together in a restaurant, that they then took a taxi to a night club and that they left the nightclub at about 10:30 and took a taxi home together. They are each other's alibis. At this point pick two students to be your suspects. Ask the two suspects to leave the room and explain that they will be interviewed by the police separately and that their stories must match.

While the two suspects are getting their stories straight divide the class into groups of three or four and explain that they are the police. Ask each group to write down between five and ten questions in the past simple to ask the suspects. For example, "What was the name of the nightclub?" "What did you eat in the restaurant?" "Who paid?" etc. After 15 minutes invite one of the suspects back into the classroom and ask her to sit in front of the police to answer their questions. When all the questions have been asked and answered, invite the second suspect back into the classroom to answer the same questions from the police. If the police manage to find three or more discrepancies in the suspects' stories, then they win. If there are only two or less then the suspects go free!

6. The last time

Language / Skill practiced: Past simple
Time: 20 mins
Language level: Pre-intermediate to intermediate

Prepare some simple questions in the past tense starting with, "When was the last time……" For example, "When was the last time you ate a hamburger?" "When was the last time you went swimming?" "When was the last time you got drunk?" "When was the last time you saw a really good movie?" etc. Write these sentences on the board or give each student a paper copy of them. Put students into pairs. Students take it in turn to ask and answer each question plus at least three more follow up questions in the past tense. For example:

S1: When was the last time you saw a really good movie?
S2: Oh, about 6 months ago
S1: What was it?
S2: Inception
S1: Oh I don't know it, where did you see it?
S2: Here, in town at the Cinema in that new shopping plaza.

And so on.

7. A story in your pocket

Language / Skill practiced: Past simple/ Past continuous / Past perfect
Time: 15 to 20 mins
Language level: Pre-intermediate to intermediate

Arrange students into a circle and ask them to place in front of them two objects they have in their pocket or bag, for example, a pen, a bit of money, an orange and so on. Include yourself in the circle too. Bring a few extra items to class as you don't really want any repetition. Begin by starting a story with two or three sentences, that must include one of the objects in front of you. The student to your left continues the story, again including an object in front of them. And so on. For example:

Teacher (has a set of keys and an mp3 player in front of her): I got home late last night and parked my car. It was raining so I ran to my front door and, oh no! I had lost my keys!

Student 1 (has a credit card and a lighter in front of him): um, I was really cold and um couldn't open the door, so I tried to open it using my credit card, you know to open the lock?

Student 2 (has a dictionary and a cuddly toy in front of her): yes, so I tried and tried but couldn't so, um, I, I don't know. But my cuddly toy was getting wet!

And so on.

Each student should have two objects in front of them so

the story can go round the circle two times. As a follow up you can, if you wish, ask the student to write out the story.

8. Verb challenge

Language / Skill practiced: Verb forms
Time: 15 mins
Language level: Elementary to pre-intermediate

Divide the class into pairs and give each pair a set of cards on which are written the infinitive form (without to) of any verbs you wish to practice. Students take it in turn to pick a card and read the verb to their partner who then says the past tense form. The first student must then say the past participle form. For example:

S1 (Picks a card): See
S2: Saw
S1: Seen

If you wish to introduce a scoring system, do so. I have never really found the need. You have to stay on the ball in this activity as some students may need a lot of help remembering the past and past participle forms (I'm thinking of you Big Mohammed and Little Mohammed!)

9. Irregular verbs bingo

Language / Skill practiced: Past tense irregular verbs
Time: 20 - 25 mins
Language level: Elementary to pre-intermediate

Divide the class into groups of three or four. Give each group a 5 by 5 grid in which you have written the past tense of 25 irregular verbs. Each team's grid should be slightly different. Call out the infinitive form of these verbs. Students mark their grid when they hear one of their words. The first team to get a row of five words horizontally, vertically or diagonally, calls out "Bingo!" and upon verification from you, is declared the winner.

10. Past participle pelmanism

Language / Skill practiced: Past participles
Time: 15 mins
Language level: Elementary to pre-intermediate

Write, on a piece of card an infinitive verb. On another write its past participle form. Continue until you have a set of 20 or so pairs. You need one set for each group of three students.

Divide the class into groups of three and give each group a set of cards and ask them to lay them face down on the desk in front of them, infinitive verbs to the left and their past participle forms to the right. Students take it in turns to pick up a card from the left, say the verb, and then pick a card from the right and say the past participle form. If these two cards are a match e.g. "see" and "seen" then they keep the cards and have another go. If not then they must replace the cards in exactly the same place, and it is the next student's turn. Continue until all the pairs have been found. Add up who has the most pairs to declare a winner.

11. Are you experienced?

Language / Skill practiced: Past simple / Present perfect
Time: 20 mins
Language level: Elementary to intermediate

Prepare a list of interesting, "Have you ever .." questions. For example, "Have you ever been scuba diving?" "Have you ever ridden a camel?" and so on. Put students into pairs to ask and answer the questions. When they receive an affirmative reply they then ask a further 5 questions in the past simple. For example:

S1: Have you ever been scuba diving?
S2: No, I haven't.
S1: Oh, Ok. Have you ever ridden a camel?
S2: Yes, I have.
S1: Oh really? When?
S2: Last year, when I was in Egypt.
S2: Oh, really? You went to Egypt. What was it like?

And so on. When each pair has asked and answered their questions you can, if you wish, ask them to report to the class on interesting things they have found out about their partner.

12. Hotter, hotter…

Language / Skill practiced: Present perfect
Time: 15 to 25 mins
Language level: Elementary to intermediate

Ask one student to examine the classroom carefully before leaving the room. While she is out of the room, change something in the classroom. E.g. put a student's cap on another student, change the seating position of one or two students or move the CD player to another part of the room.

When they student returns to the room she walks around the room and attempts to find out what has been changed. As she moves closer to the part of the classroom where the change occurred the other students can tell her, "hotter, hotter, really hot now!" and so on. As she moves further away from the scene of the change, the other students can tell her "colder, colder" and so on and in this way direct her to the change. When she thinks she has seen the change she can, using the present perfect tense, tell you. For example, "You have turned that table the wrong way around" or "Michael has taken of his coat." Repeat with a new student.

13. My perfect life

Language / Skill practiced: Present perfect / Present perfect continuous tense
Time: 20 mins
Language level: Pre-intermediate to intermediate

Ask each student to write down three sentences about themselves using the present perfect / present perfect continuous tense and for / since. For example, "I have been living in the city for three years. I have loved football since I was a little girl. I have been married since November." Ask them to add their name to the bottom of the piece of paper before collecting them all up. Now either you, or one of your students, read out the sentences on the pieces of paper one by one. The other students attempt to guess who wrote the sentences.

14. Find a classmate who....

Language / Skill practiced: Present simple
Time: 15 to 20 mins
Language level: Elementary to pre-intermediate

Prepare a list of ten, "Find some one who…" sentences, all in the present simple tense. For example, "Find someone who gets up before six o'clock," "Find someone who drinks more than five cups of coffee a day," etc. Give each student a copy of this list.

Students stand up and try to find a student for each of

their sentences by asking questions to their classmates. For example, "Do you get up before six, Daniel? No? Ok. Do you get up before six, Sofia? Yes, Great. Thank you" They then write down the students name next to the corresponding sentence.

After 10 minutes or so stop the activity and ask students to sit down in groups of 4. They then tell their group members what they found out. For example, "Well, Sofia gets up before six. Ahmed drinks about ten cups of coffee a day! Pedro…" and so on.

15. Frequency predictions

Language / Skill practiced: Present simple / Adverbs and expressions of frequency
Time: 15 mins
Language level: Elementary to pre-intermediate

Prepare sets of cards on which you have written adverbs and expressions of frequency, such as "sometimes," "often," "once a week" and so on. Divide the class into pairs and give each pair a set of cards face down. Students take it in turns to pick a card from the pack and ask their partner a question in order to elicit the word on the card. For example:

S1 (Picks card that says always): How often do you brush your teeth in the morning.
S2: Usually.
S1: Really! Ok, um. How often do you drink beer in the evening?
S2: Always. I always drink beer.

S1: Great, you got it. Your turn.

I've never felt the need to instigate a scoring system with this activity.

16. A question of habit

Language / Skill practiced: Present Simple / Adverbs of frequency
Time: 15 to 20 mins
Language level: Elementary to pre-intermediate

Revise adverbs of frequency with the class before writing a list of prompts on the board. For example, "Go to bed late," "Drink beer in the evening," "Go for a run in the morning" and so on.
Students work in pairs asking, "How often do you + prompt?" For example:

S1: How often do you go to bed late?
S2: I often go to bed late, well after eleven. How often do you drink beer in the evening?
S1: Not very often. I don't like the taste.

And so on. If you choose, place the class into groups when the activity is over to report on what they have found out about their partners. For example, "Jose never goes to bed late. His mum doesn't let him and he never drinks beer for the same reason…"

17. Who is it?

Language / Skill practiced: Present Simple / Describing people
Time: 15 mins
Language level: Elementary to pre-intermediate

Ask each student to write a physical description of themselves on a piece of paper. For example, "I am tall and very handsome. I am slim and have big muscles. My eyes are green and I have short dark hair." And so on. Ensure that the students do not show their descriptions to other students. Gather up the pieces of paper and read them out one by one. The class tries to guess who wrote the description. Often a student's self image is very different to the way the class sees him!

18. Carrot

Language / Skill practiced: Question forms
Time: 10 mins
Language level: Elementary to intermediate

Put students into pairs. Student 1 thinks of a verb. Student 2 asks Yes / No questions to try and fine out what the verb is but uses the word, "carrot" to replace any verb. For example:

S1: Do you carrot in the morning?
S2: Yes
S1: Do you carrot everyday?

S2: Um, yes.
S1: Drink coffee?
S2: No
S1: Do you carrot in the bathroom?
S2: Yes
S1: Ah, brush your teeth!
S2: Yes, you got it.

Students now swap roles.

19. Ask me anything

Language / Skill practiced: Question forms
Time: 20 mins
Language level: Elementary to intermediate

Select a student to come to the front of the class and sit facing the class. The other students in the class ask him any questions they like in an attempt to get him to say "yes" or "no." The student sitting facing the class must answer the questions truthfully but not say "yes" or "no." For example:

S1: Do you like football?
S2: Of course, it is our national sport.
S3: Do you watch it a lot?
S2: Not a lot, but I do watch it.
S3: I think your favourite player is Rooney, yes?
S2: No! I mean, arggh.

The student who elicited a yes or no answer, in this case S3, now sits in front of the class to answer questions.

20. Give me a question

Language / Skill practiced: Question forms
Time: 15 to 20 mins
Language level: Elementary to upper-intermediate

Prepare a list of answers based around several topics. For example: Geography, History, Sport and so on. Divide the class into groups of three or four. Call out the answers and award points for correct questions and minus points for incorrect questions. For example:

Teacher: Ok this one is geography. Here we go: The Nile.
Student: What is the longest river in the world?
Teacher: Correct. Well done. One point for your team. Ok second question. This is a history one: 1918
Student: When was the first world war?
Teacher: Hmm, Not quite. Sorry, your team loses a point.
Student: When did the First World War start?
Teacher: Nope. Minus one point.

And so on. (When did the First World War finish, by the way.)

21. Sausages

Language / Skill practiced: Question forms
Time: 15 mins
Language level: Elementary to intermediate

Select one student to come to the front of the class and sit down. The rest of the class can ask this student any questions they like. She must always respond with the word "sausages" but never giggle, laugh or smile. They usually don't last long! For example:

S1: How are you?
S2: Sausages
S3: What's your name?
S2: Sausages
S3: You are very handsome, aren't you?

S2: Sausages
S1: How did you get to school today?
S2: Sausages (student smiles)
S1: Ah, you smiled!

Continue with a new student answering the questions.

22. Dead or alive

Language / Skill practiced: Question forms
Time: 15 mins
Language level: Elementary to advanced

Play as a full class or in groups of four or five. One person thinks of a famous person, dead or alive. The other students have 20 Yes / No questions to find out who this person is. For example:

S2: Is this person alive?
S1: Yes, he or she is.
S3: Is it a man?
S1: Yes he is
S4: Is he a politician?
S1: No, he isn't

And so on.

23. Who am I?

Language / Skill practiced: Yes / No questions in various tenses
Time: 20 mins
Language level: Pre-intermediate to advanced

Ask each student to write down the name of a famous person, dead or alive, on a piece of adhesive backed paper. They should on no account reveal the name of the person they are writing down. Ask each student to stick their piece of paper on the back of another student. Students now stand up and ask each other student three "yes / no" questions to try and work out who they are. For example:

S1: Am I alive?
S2: Yes
S1: Am I a sports person?
S2: No
S1: Am I a TV personality?
S2: Yes, you are.

And so on. After they have asked their questions ask the students to sit down and tell the class who they think they are. You can now reveal if they are correct.

24. What do you do?

Language / Skill practiced: Jobs vocabulary / Question forms

Time: 10 mins
Language level: Elementary to intermediate

Put students into pairs. Student A picks a job, for example, accountant. The other student must ask Yes / No questions to work out what the job is. For example:

S1: Ok, Do you work in a building?
S2: Yes
S1: Do you have to be very clever to do this job?
S2: Oh yes.
S1: Do you have to wear a uniform?

And so on. When the student B has guessed the job, students swap roles.

25. The extraordinarily long sentence

Language / Skill practiced: Sentence formation
Time: 10 mins
Language level: Elementary to intermediate

Arrange the students in a circle. Write the word, "The" on the board and explain it is the first word in a sentence. Each student takes it in turn to add one word to the sentence, for example, "elephant," "walked," "into" and so on. When a student can't think of a word or adds a word you deem grammatically incorrect, they are "out," and the game continues without them. The winner is the last student who remains.

26. Three in a row

Language / Skill practiced: Sentence formation
Time: 15 mins
Language level: Beginner to elementary

Draw a simple tic tac toe, or noughts and crosses, grid on the board, and in each of the nine spaces, write a piece of vocabulary you wish to revise with the class. Divide the class into two teams. Ask the first team to pick a word from the grid and make a grammatically correct sentence using it. If they manage to do this successfully, replace the word with an "X." It is now the other teams turn to pick a word and make a sentence with it. If they do this successfully, replace the word with a "O." Continue until one team, the winners, have three "X's" or "O's" in a row.

27. Sentence jumble

Language / Skill practiced: Sentence formation
Time: 15 to 30 mins
Language level: Elementary to pre-intermediate

Divide the class into groups of three and give each group three sentences on pieces of card or paper, containing whatever language you are studying with the class, cut up into their component words. Students arrange the words to make the original sentences. When all the groups have finished, check their work before collecting the cut up sentences and redistributing to another group.

28. What am I doing?

Language / Skill practiced: Present continuous questions forms
Time: 15 mins
Language level: Elementary to pre-intermediate

Prepare, on pieces of card, a set of approximately 20 verbs that you'd like your students to practice. Put the students into groups of threes. One student takes a card and acts out the verb while the other two students try to guess the verb using full present continuous questions. For example:

S2: Are you cooking?
S1: No
S2: Are you washing your hands?
S1: No
S3: Are you doing the washing up?
S1: Yes, That's right!

The student who correctly guesses the verb now picks a card and acts out a new verb, and so on.

29. How am I doing it?

Language / Skill practiced: Present continuous questions forms / Adverbs of action
Time: 15 mins
Language level: Elementary to pre-intermediate

Prepare, on pieces of card, a list of approximately 20 adverbs that you'd like your students to practice. Divide the class into groups of three. One student takes a card. The other students assign him an action, for example, "washing up." This student must perform the action in the manner of the adverb, for example, slowly, happily, quickly and so on. The other students attempt to guess the adverb using full present continuous questions. For example:

S2: Are you washing up happily?
S1: No!
S3: Are you washing up quickly?
S1: Yes, but that's not it.
S3: I know, angrily!
S1: Yes that's right.

The student who correctly guesses the adverb now picks a card, is assigned an action, performs the action in the manner of the adverb and so on.

30. Small talk

Language / Skill practiced: Various / Fluency skills

Time: 15 mins
Language level: Pre-intermediate to upper-intermediate

Elicit the concept of small talk from your students and write up some of the common topics on the board e.g. weather, sport, TV etc. Elicit some common questions for each topic and write these on the board also. For example, "Nice weather we're having isn't it?" and "Did you see the game last night?" etc. Divide students into pairs and ask them to engage in small talk for five minutes. After 5 minutes students stop and find a new partner to repeat the activity. After a further 5 minutes stop the activity and ask two or more pairs to demonstrate their ability to make small talk to the class.

31. Quick debates

Language / Skill practiced: Various / Fluency skills
Time: 15 mins
Language level: Intermediate to advanced

Divide the class into pairs. Give each group a pack of cards. On one side of each card should be a contentious statement such as, "The death penalty is inhuman," or "Dogs shouldn't be allowed in cities." On the other side should be a plus or minus mark. Plus means agree and minus means disagree. Students take it in turns to pick a card, read the statement and then either claim to agree or disagree, giving supporting reasons and evidence, depending on the mark on the card. His partner must then guess whether they really do agree or disagree with the statement. If they guess correctly then they take the card from their partner and keep it. If they guess incorrectly, then the first student keeps the card. For example:

S1 (picks a card with a plus sign on one side): Ok. The statement is: Nuclear power is the best way to solve the world's energy crisis. I actually do agree with this. Look at a country like France. They use a lot of nuclear energy and for the most part it is cheap and safe. We can't continue to burn coal because its bad for the environment and solar power just isn't efficient or cheap enough. It's the only realistic way forwards.
S2: hmm. You sound convincing but we all know it's very dangerous and I just don't think you're telling the truth. Lie.
S1: Actually I'm not lying. I do think it's the best way. (S1 keeps the card.) Your go!

When all cards are gone, they can add up who has the most cards and declare a winner.

32. Survival situation

Language / Skill practiced: Various / Fluency skills
Time: 25 to 30 mins
Language level: Intermediate to advanced

Divide the class into groups of four or five students. Explain to the groups that they have just survived an airplane crash in the middle of the jungle. They will have to trek through the jungle to the coast, about 150 kilometers away. They've managed to salvage 20 items from the airplane. These are: a small pen knife, a three-liter water bottle full of water, some salt tablets, a piece of rope, a mirror, a parachute, a life jacket, five small bottles of whiskey, a live chicken, a fully charged mobile phone (no reception as yet), a saw, a long piece of hollow bamboo, some nails, some insect repellent, a lighter, a jar of coffee, a small portable gas stove with gas canister, a basic first aid kit, a big faithful dog, and five sleeping bags. Unfortunately they can only carry eight items with them (5 sleeping bags count as one item as does the whiskey.)

Each group must decide amongst themselves which of the twenty items they will take with them and why. After 25 minutes, stop the activity and ask each group, in turn, to explain to the class which items they have chosen and why.

33. Dice talking

Language / Skill practiced: Various / Fluency skills
Time: 20 to 25 mins
Language level: Elementary to intermediate

Divide the class into groups of three of four and issue each group with two dice. Write on the board the numbers 2 to 12 and topics / structures you would like students to discuss next to the numbers. For example:

2: Things that scare me (present simple)
3: A happy day I had (narrative tenses)
4: What I'm going to do tomorrow (going to)

And so on. Students take it in turns to throw the dice and speak for 1 minute on the topic their number represents. When they have finished each student asks them one (or more) question about their short speech.

34. Experts

Language / Skill practiced: Various / Fluency skills
Time: 40 to 50 mins
Language level: Pre-intermediate to upper-intermediate

Ask each student to think of something they know a lot about. This can be absolutely anything, for example, "David Beckham," "Computers," "How to lose weight," or "The history of New Zealand."

Ask them to write their topic on a piece of card, fold it and place it in front of them so that everyone can see their topic. Divide the class down the middle into A and B and ask students from A to think of and write down some questions to ask the experts from B and vice versa. Ask them to write down at least one question for each student. After 15 minutes ask the students from A to stand up and approach the experts in B in order to ask their questions and any follow up questions they may have. When they have finished they return to their seats and the students in B stand up to ask their questions to the experts in A. When all questions have been asked put the students into groups of three to tell each other the most interesting things they have learned.

35. Don't stop talking

Language / Skill practiced: Various / Fluency skills
Time: 15 mins
Language level: Elementary to pre-intermediate

Invite students one by one to come to the front of the class and sit in a chair facing the class. Announce a topic, for example, "yourself," "sports" or "holidays." The student must then talk for as long as possible on this topic without pausing for more than one second. In addition, it is a good idea to dictate that fillers such as "Uh" and "Um" are regarded as pausing. Time the students and declare the student who manages to talk for the longest the winner.

This activity doesn't take as long as you might think, as students, in my experience, find it really difficult especially with the added pressure of speaking to the whole class.

36. The goat, the tiger and the cabbage

Language / Skill practiced: Various / Fluency skills
Time: 15 mins
Language level: Pre–intermediate to upper intermediate

Draw a simple picture of a river on the board. Draw a goat, a cabbage, a tiger and a farmer on one side of the river. Label them if your drawing skills are anything like as bad as mine! In the river on the same side as the farmer et al., draw a boat. Explain to the students that the farmer has to get his animals and cabbage across the river in the boat. But he can only take one thing at a time. In addition explain that if left alone, the goat will eat the cabbage and the tiger will eat the goat. Divide the class into groups of three or four and ask them to discuss the situation and solve the problem. After 15 minutes stop the activity and ask each group to tell the class their solution.

The correct solution is: The farmer takes the goat across the river. Leaves it there and comes back for the tiger takes the tiger across and takes the goat back. He then takes the cabbage across, leaves it with the tiger and goes back to finally take the goat over for the second time.

37. Find out about me

Language / Skill practiced: Various / Fluency skills
Time: 15 mins
Language level: Elementary to intermediate

Ask students to write down on a piece of paper, 10 answers about themselves. For example, "1982," "3," "watching movies and reading," "Tom Cruise," "for ten years," "James," "Indian," "smoking," "fish," and "to be really rich." Put students into pairs and ask them to swap pieces of paper and to ask questions based on what their partner has written. The goal is to get all ten questions correct. For example:

S1: When were you born?
S2: 1982

S1: Great got one. Um, what are your hobbies?
S2: Watching movies and reading.
S1: Good. Who's your favourite film star?
S2: Jennifer Lawrence
S1: Oh, ok. Which film star do you hate?
S2: Correct, Tom Cruise.

Continue for ten minutes or until all the questions have been asked. Then ask students to tell the class a little that they have found out about their partner.

38. What do we have in common?

Language / Skill practiced: Various / Fluency skills
Time: 10 to 15 mins
Language level: Pre-intermediate to advanced

Divide the class into pairs. The objective? To find three things they have in common with their partner. For example:

S1: I like ice cream. What about you?
S2: No, not really. But I do eat a lot of chocolate. Do you?
S1: Yes, I do. Great. That's one. How about exercise. Do you go running?...
And so on.
To make the activity more challenging you can ask students to stick to a particular topic, for example, "Mornings," "the Internet" or "recycling" For example,
S1: Ok, um the internet. Um I use it a lot to look at sports results. How about you?
S2: No, not really. I don't like sport, but I do download a

lot of movies.
S1: Me too! Ok, we need two more.

And so on. When all student s have found three things in common you can ask them to report back to the class on their findings.

39. Student line up

Language / Skill practiced: Various / Fluency skills
Time: 15 mins
Language level: Elementary to intermediate

For this activity to work correctly it is imperative that students use only English, not their native language, so remind them sternly before you start.

Ask students to stand up. Ask them to arrange themselves in a line from youngest to oldest. This of course means they need to use the question, "How old are you?" and various other language to arrange themselves, such as "No you should stand there" and "I should be next to Jose" etc. Continue repeating the activity, gradually increasing the difficulty of the task. For example, "From student who did best at school to worst at school" "From student who is the most self confident to least self confident" and so on. As the complexity of the task increases so does the greater variety of vocabulary and structures the students are forced to use.

40. The Seven Wonders

Language / Skill practiced: Various / Fluency skills
Time: 15 mins
Language level: Pre-intermediate to advanced

Elicit from students what some of the ancient wonders of the world are and which people made the list (the ancient Greeks.) It's unlikely that they'll be able to list more than two or three (can you?) so have a list handy that you can project onto the board or hand out. Now divide the class into groups of three or four and explain that they are going to make their own list of the Seven Wonders of the World but with the caveat that at least one person in the group must have seen this wonder. Obviously this limits them from the usual suspects and encourages them to be imaginative. Stress that they must be able to explain why they have chosen the wonders they did.

When everyone has finished ask one person from each group to stand up and list her group's wonders and why they had them on the list. If you choose you can then ask the class as a whole to choose the best seven wonders mentioned.

41. The truth or a dirty lie?

Language / Skill practiced: Various / Fluency skills
Time: 30 mins
Language level: Pre-intermediate to advanced

Ask students to write down, on a sheet of paper, three sentences about themselves, two of which are true and one a lie. For example, "I lived in Italy for two years when I was younger," "I can juggle" and "I drink 10 cups of coffee a day." Put students into pairs and ask them to swap their pieces of paper. Both students must pretend that all the sentences they wrote are true. Students take turns to question their partner to try and determine which is a lie. For example:

S1 (reading S2's first sentence): I lived in Italy for two years when I was younger. Hmm. Why were you in Italy?
S2: My Dad had a job there.
S1: What did he do?
S2: Um, um a doctor, he was a doctor!
S1: Really? Are there a lot of Japanese doctors working in Italy?
S2: Um, yes. I think so.
S1: Hmmm. Ok, next sentence

When each student has had a chance to question his partner about her sentences, ask them to make a guess as to which sentence of their partner's is a lie.

42. Classroom theater

Language / Skill practiced: Various
Time: 25-30 mins
Language level: Pre-intermediate to advanced

Divide the class into pairs and give each pair the start of a dialogue. For example:

A Domestic Dispute
Terry: I can't believe you burnt my dinner again.
June: Well I did. Maybe you should do the cooking for a change!
Terry: I would but I'm at work all day.
June: You think I don't work! I…….

Or

A First Date
James: You look very pretty.
Lisa: Oh thank you. You have such a sweet tongue.
James: No! I mean it, anyway shall we get going.
Lisa: Sure! Do you have a car.
James: No, but it's a wonderful evening. I thought we could walk. You know; you, me the moonlight……

Ask the students to continue the dialogue for at least another 10 lines and then to practice and memorize their conversation. After 20 minutes or when you think everyone is ready, invite the pairs to come to the front and act out their short sketch to the class.

43. Odd one out

Language / Skill practiced: Vocabulary
Time: 15 to 20 mins
Language level: Elementary to advanced

Divide the class into groups of three or four. Write four words on the board, three of which belong to a group and the other, "The odd one out." For example, "Fat," "Happy," "Kind" and Teacher." The first team to raise a hand gets to try and guess the answer. For example:

T: Yes, Roberto?
S1: Fat is the odd one out because the other words are nice.
T: No, sorry Roberto. Good try though but no points for your team. Yes, Paula?
S1: Teacher is the odd one out because it is a person and the others describe a person
T: Yes, that's right. The others are all adjectives. One point for you team.

Write up four more words and repeat. Now ask each team to think of four words with an odd one out. Each team then takes it in turn to write their words on the board and invite the other team to guess the odd one out. This activity can be used with students up to an advanced level but obviously you have to make it a bit trickier. You could use, for example, "Peanut," "walnut," "brazil nut" and "hazel nut." (The peanut isn't actually a nut.)

44. Vocabulary swap

Language / Skill practiced: Vocabulary
Time: 15 to 20 mins
Language level: Elementary to intermediate

Issue each student with a slip of paper on which you have written a word you wish to introduce or revise and its definition. Students stand up and take turns reading the definition to a partner who can either guess the word or simply say, "I don't know." After both students have read and heard the definitions, they swap slips of paper and find a new partner to repeat the activity. For example:

S1: Confused or uncertain
S2: Perplexed, right?
S1: Yes.
S2: Ok my one. Not busy; not occupied.
S1: I don't know.
S2: It's, "Idle." (Students now swap their pieces of paper and find a new partner.)

Continue until all the students can guess all the words from their definitions.

45. What am I drawing?

Language / Skill practiced: Vocabulary
Time: 15 mins
Language level: Beginner to pre-intermediate

Divide the class into two teams and ask each team to stand together facing the board. Ask one person from each team to come to the board. Give them each a pen and a slip of paper with a word appropriate to their language level on it. As quickly as they can each student must draw the word on the board for their team to guess. The team which guesses the quickest gets one point. Repeat with new students from each team. Obviously nouns are the easiest words to draw but verbs and adjectives are also possible, and fun!

46. Vocabulary race

Language / Skill practiced: Vocabulary
Time: 10 to 15 mins
Language level: Elementary to intermediate

Divide the class into two or three teams and ask each team to stand in a line facing the board, about ten feet away if your classroom is big enough. Issue each team a board marker. Tell the class a topic you would like to focus on, for example, "Capital Cities." The student at the front of each line runs to the board and writes one word related to your topic, for example, "Paris" or, "London." She then runs back to her team hands the pen to the next student at the front of the line before taking her place at the back of the line. The student holding the pen runs to the board, writes another word, heads back to his team, hands over the pen and goes to the back of the line. And so on.

Continue for two minutes before stopping the activity and awarding each team a point for each correct word and taking away points for incorrect words and spelling mistakes etc. Repeat with a new topic.

47. Word association

Language / Skill practiced: Vocabulary
Time: 15 mins
Language level: Elementary to intermediate

Put students into pairs. Students take it in turns to say the first word that comes to mind. The only rule is that they must be able to say what connection this word has to the previous word within 5 seconds if challenged. If they can't, then they lose one point. For example:

S1: Elephant
S2: Tiger
S1: Africa
S2: Spain
S1: oil
S2: What? Challenge.
S1: There is lots of olive oil in Spain
S2: Oh ok, one point to you. Fry.
S1: TV.

S2: Challenge!

And so on. The scoring really isn't that important in this game, it is more that the students are using English to justify their choice of words.

48. What does it mean?

Language / Skill practiced: Vocabulary / 3rd person singular verb ending (mean/z/)
Time: 15 mins
Language level: Elementary to pre-intermediate

Give each student a slip of paper and ask them to write a word, in their native language, on it. Ask students to stand up and find a partner. Each student asks his partner the question, "What does word on paper mean?" To which the response is either, "I don't know" or "It means word in English." For example:

S1: What does "hola" mean?
S2: It means "hello"
S1: Yes, correct!

Or

S1: What does "hola" mean?
S2: Um, I don't know.
S1: It means "hello"

When each student has asked and answered a question they swap their slips of paper and find a new partner.

49. Topics

Language / Skill practiced: Vocabulary
Time: 15 mins
Language level: Elementary to pre-intermediate

Divide the class into groups of three or four. Announce a topic, for example, "Animals." Each group takes it in turn to say an animal (no repetition!). The first group who cannot think of an animal in 5 secs are out and the game continues without them. Continue eliminating groups until you have one team remaining, the winners! Repeat with a new topic. For example: (Topic is clothes)

Group 1: pants
Group 2: shirt
Group 3: shoes
Group 1: sweater
Group 2: Um, Um, shirt!
Teacher: No, someone said that 3, 2, 1: Ok your out
Group 3: hat

And so on.

50. ABC topics

Language / Skill practiced: Vocabulary
Time: 15 mins
Language level: Elementary to pre-intermediate

As above, but announce both a topic and a first letter. For example, "Animals" and "A." Each group takes it in turn to say an animal beginning with the letter A e.g. alligator, aardvark, antelope, ant, aphid and so on.

51. Chain spelling

Language / Skill practiced: Vocabulary / Spelling
Time: 15 mins
Language level: Beginner to pre-intermediate

Arrange the class into a circle. Announce a word. Each student takes it in turn to say one letter of the word in the correct order. When a student says the wrong letter she loses one point. After losing three points she is, "out," and the game continues without her. The last student to remain is the winner. For example:

Teacher: Ok, um, "Ostrich"
S1 O
S2: S
S3: T
S4: R
S5: E
Teacher: No sorry, minus one point for you.
S6: I
S7: C
S8: H
Teacher: Ok great, new word, and remember Salma you are on minus one point, ok? Right, um, "Desperate."

52. Constantinople

Language / Skill practiced: Vocabulary / Spelling
Time: 5 to 10 mins
Language level: Elementary to pre-intermediate

Divide the class into pairs. Write the word Constantinople, or any other long word on the board. Students write down, in two minutes as many words as they can think of using only the letters from the word. For example, "Cat," "tin," "noise" and so on. After two minutes stop the activity and award one point for each correctly spelled word, two points for any four letter words, three points for any five letter words and so on.

53. Anagrams

Language / Skill practiced: Vocabulary / Spelling
Time: 15 mins
Language level: Elementary to intermediate

Divide the class into teams of three or four. Write an anagram of a word on the board, for example, "rvceel." The first team to correctly guess the word, "clever" wins one point for their team. Continue with four more words. Now ask each team to prepare five anagrams of their own, and to then come to the front of the class, write their anagrams on the board. Award a point to each team that correctly guesses each one. Alternatively have them simply give their anagrams on a piece of paper to another team to work out the words.

54. Donkey

Language / Skill practiced: Vocabulary / Spelling
Time: 30 to 40 mins
Language level: Intermediate to advanced

A truly excellent game with somewhat complex rules! Write on the board, "You CAN NOT finish a word." Put students into groups of three. Explain that each group will take it in turns to say a letter. They cannot finish a word but must be thinking of a word in case they are challenged. For example:

Group 1: C
Group 2: A
Group 3: (Don't want to say T as this will make / finish a word and they will lose) A
Group 1: Challenge!

Group 3 can't think of a word starting with the letter CAA and so they lose! However, if Group 1 were to challenge and Group 3 could think of a word beginning CAA then Group 1 would lose. So for example:

Group 1: c
Group 2: u
Group 3: l
Group 1: Challenge!
Group 3: Cult!

And so Group 1 loses. When a team lose once, assign them the letter D. When they lose again, assign them the letters DO and so on until one team is a DONKEY. The losers! For practical reason exclude two letter words from the rule, "You can't finish a word."

55. What's in the bag?

Language / Skill practiced: Vocabulary / Spelling
Time: 10 mins
Language level: Elementary to intermediate

Bring into class a bag filled with 20 or so different objects. Take the objects out of the bag one by one stating what they are as you place them on the table. For example, "An apple. I might eat that later. A pen, a book I'm reading, some sellotape I found in the teachers' room, my lighter…" and so on. Replace all the items in the bag and divide the class into pairs to write down as many of the items as they can remember. After two minutes, stop the activity and award each pair one point for each item they managed to remember and spell correctly down.

56. Extremely long words

Language / Skill practiced: Vocabulary / Spelling
Time: 15 to 20 mins
Language level: Elementary to pre-intermediate

Divide the class into two teams. Write a word such as, "turnip." horizontally on the board. Explain that this word is worth six points because it contains six letters. Divide the class into two teams, A and B. Invite team A to think of the longest word they can that begins with the last letter of the word, "turnip," for example, "practically" and write this vertically on the board using the "p" of turnip as the first letter. Team B must now think of a long word starting with the last letter of the word, "practically," for example, "yesterday." Write this horizontally on the board using the "y" of practically as the first letter. Continue in this way until you've run out of space and then add up all the vertical letters and then all the horizontal letters to give each team their score and declare a winner.

57. Clap spelling

Language / Skill practiced: Spelling
Time: 15 mins
Language level: Elementary to pre-intermediate

Arrange the class in a circle and ask them to begin clapping in a steady, two beat rhythm. Now call out a word, for example, "strange." The students must, in turn and between claps, call out the correct letters in sequence to spell the word. For example:

(all students clapping): Clap Clap
S1: S
Clap Clap
S2: T
Clap Clap
S3: R
Clap Clap
S4: A
Clap Clap
S5: N
Clap Clap

S6:G
Clap Clap
S7:E
Increase the tempo and call out a new word and continue. If you wish you can use a scoring system to deduct points from students for mistakes, but I've found the game fun enough without this as long as you keep increasing the clapping speed and call out words appropriate to the students' level.

58. Crosswords construction

Language / Skill practiced: Vocabulary / Definitions / Synonyms / Antonyms
Time: 30 to 45 mins
Language level: Pre-intermediate to advanced

Prepare several different crossword grids showing ONLY the answers, not the questions. These answers should focus on vocabulary you wish to revise. Divide the class into groups of three or four and give each group one of these crossword grids with answers. Each group now copies the grid, without answers, and writes questions for each of the answers you originally wrote in. When each group has finished writing their questions hand their crossword to another group to complete.

59. Hot seat

Language / Skill practiced: Vocabulary / Synonyms / Antonyms / Definitions
Time: 20 mins
Language level: Elementary to upper-intermediate

Divide the class into groups of four or five. Ask one student from each team to come to the front of the class and sit in a chair with its back to the board, the hot seat. Each student's team members can gather around her. Write a word you would like to revise on the board. Each team must attempt to describe this word to their team member who is sitting in the chair without using the word itself. For example:

S1: It's an adjective to describe a person
S2 (in chair): Fat!
S3: No, about their feelings.
S2: Happy?
S1: No, um. It's the opposite of interested.
S2: Um, excited?
S1: No! The opposite!

The student who guesses first wins one point for their team. Repeat with new words, or even sentences, and with new team members in the chairs.

60. Password

Language / Skill practiced: Vocabulary / Definitions / Synonyms / Antonyms
Time: 15 to 20 mins
Language level: Elementary to intermediate

Write words you would like your students to revise on pieces of card. Divide the class into groups of four and give each group a set of cards. One student takes a card from the top of the pile and explains what the word is without saying the word itself. The student who correctly guesses the word takes the next card from the pile and explains the new word. For example:

Student 1: It's an adjective. Umm, how you feel on a sunny day.
Student 2: happy?
Student 1: No, um. Opposite of cold
Student 3: Hot?
Student 1: Yes correct. Your go.

61. Password prohibition

Language / Skill practiced: Vocabulary / Definitions / Synonyms / Antonyms
Time: 15 to 20 mins
Language level: Pre-intermediate to advanced

As above, but on each card write three additional words that the student can't say. If the word is "hot," for example, you might choose to write the words, "cold," "sun" and "feel." This makes this game more difficult and suitable for more advanced students.

62. Definition bluff

Language / Skill practiced: Vocabulary / Definitions / Synonyms / Antonyms
Time: 25-30 mins
Language level: Elementary to pre-intermediate

Divide the class into teams of three or four. Give each team a dictionary and a word written on a piece of paper. This word should be new to the students. The students in each group must now find out the meaning of the word you have given them and prepare three written definitions for it, two false and one the true definition. When each team has finished writing, ask them to read out their word and its three definitions. The other teams then try and guess which the true definition is. Award one point to any team that correctly guesses the true definition.

63. Sentence song

Language / Skill practiced: Vocabulary / Listening skills
Time: 20 mins
Language level: Elementary to intermediate

Print out the lyrics to a song you think your class would like. Ballads tend to work best. Put the class into groups of three or four and give each group a copy of the lyrics but cut up into sentences (or words if you wish to make it really difficult.) Students listen to the song and arrange their sentences into the correct order. Play the song again so that students can check their work.

64. Tape-recorder dictation

Language / Skill practiced: Listening skills
Time: 15 mins
Language level: Elementary to intermediate

It's possible you may have to explain what a tape recorder is to your class! Or simply call it CD player dictation. Draw on the board a "play" symbol, a "rewind" symbol, a "forwards" symbol and a "stop" or "pause" symbol. Elicit what each of the symbols are. Now explain that the students are going to take down some dictation. You will read the dictation but you are a tape recorder and respond exactly like a tape recorder. Begin speaking at a normal pace when a student says "play." Almost immediately they will start falling behind and should call "stop," then "rewind." Continue following their directions exactly until they have completed the dictation. A lot of fun!

65. Whispered sentences

Language / Skill practiced: Listening skills
Time: 15 mins
Language level: Beginner to pre-intermediate

First check that the class is familiar with the concept of whispering. Arrange the class into two teams and into two lines. Write down a sentence on a piece of paper, for example, "John got up and decided to eat some lovely cherries." Show the piece of paper to the student at the head of each line. This student whispers the sentence to the student next to him who then whispers the sentence to the student next to her and so on until the student at the end of the line has heard the sentence. Ask the student at the end of each line what sentence they heard and award points to the team who got closest to the original meaning.

66. Aliens

Language / Skill practiced: Language of description / Relative clauses
Time: 5 to 10 mins
Language level: Elementary to pre-intermediate

Put students into pairs. One student plays the part of an alien, a being from another planet. This alien doesn't know what any of the earth objects are and wants to find out about them by asking questions of his partner. For example:

S1 (The alien): What's this?
S2: It's a cup.
S1: What's a cup?
S2: It's something that you drink from.
S1: What does drink mean?
S2: It means when you put liquid into your body
S1: What's liquid?
S2: Um, fluid, like water or coffee.

And so on. Students can swap roles and / or partners one or more times.

67. Shouting dictation

Language / Skill practiced: Listening skills / Reading skills
Time: 20 mins
Language level: Elementary to intermediate

Put students into pairs facing each other but sitting on opposite sides of the room. Give one student from each pair a text appropriate to the class's language level. Use several different texts. This student should dictate their text to their partner who writes down what she hears. The resulting noise of half of the class speaking at once will mean students have to speak extremely loudly and clearly for their partner to understand. After 10 minutes stop the activity and mark the texts based on how much they have written, accuracy and spelling. Ask students to swap roles and repeat.

68. Running dictation

Language / Skill practiced: Listening skills / Reading skills
Time: 15 mins
Language level: Elementary to intermediate

Divide the class into pairs and ask each pair to sit together at the same end of the classroom. On the opposite wall pin a text appropriate to your students' language level. One student from each pair should run to the text, memorize as many sentences as he can, run back to his partner and repeat the sentences for his partner to write down. He then runs back to the text to memorize the next sentences, back to his partner and so on. Award points to the first, second and third pair to finish and then stop the activity. Take away points from each team for spelling mistakes, missing words etc. and then announce the winner.

69. Proverb match

Language / Skill practiced: Listening / Reading skills / Proverbs
Time: 15 mins
Language level: Intermediate to advanced

Prepare some proverbs on slips of paper before class. For example, "Every cloud has a silver lining," "two wrongs don't make a right" and so on. Cut the proverbs in half and distribute to the class so that every student has one half of a proverb. Students now circulate around the classroom reading their half of the proverb until they find the student with the other half. Ask students to sit down with this person and two other pairs. In their groups of six they read their proverbs to each other and try and work out the meaning. After 5 minutes stop the class and ask each group to read out their proverbs and to tell the class the meaning. Correct students where necessary.

Now, in the same groups, ask students to think of proverbs in their native language and to translate them into English. Each group, in turn, then reads out their translated proverb and explains the meaning.

70. Student story order

Language / Skill practiced: Reading / Listening skills
Time: 15 mins
Language level: Elementary to pre-intermediate

Prepare a short story in the past tense appropriate to the level of your students. Alternatively use a text from your course book. Cut this text into as many sections as you have students; ideally, one sentence per student. Give each student their sentence or short passage and ask them to stand up. Students MUST NOT show their sentence to any students. Students read out their sentences and arrange themselves in a line corresponding to the correct order of sentences in the story.

71. Looking for love

Language / Skill practiced: Reading skills/ Writing skills
Time: 20 to 30 mins
Language level: Pre-intermediate to advanced

Elicit or explain the concept of a lonely hearts column. Show your students some examples copied from a newspaper or written yourself. Ask some general comprehension and vocabulary questions. Now give your students 15 minutes to work individually to write their own lonely hearts ad complete with a fake name. Collect these up and then pin then to the wall. Students can now stand up, read their classmate's lonely hearts ads and choose one to reply to. Give students another 15 minutes to do this. Collect up the replies and act as the postman to deliver these to the correct students. Ask two or three students to read out the letters they received to the class.

72. Superlative students

Language / Skill practiced: Superlative adjectives
Time: 15 mins
Language level: Pre-intermediate to upper-intermediate

Put students into groups of three or four. Each group writes three superlative sentences about one other student in the class. Encourage them to be as inventive as possible. For example, "He isn't the most handsome in the class, but he has the nicest smile. He dresses in the nicest clothes. He has the largest ears." When each group has finished ask them to read out their sentences for the other students to listen to and guess who is being described.

73. Comparative students

Language / Skill practiced: Comparative adjectives
Time: 15 mins
Language level: Pre-intermediate to upper-intermediate

As above, except that students instead write comparative sentences. For example, "This person is taller than Ahmed but not taller than Mohommed. This person has a bigger nose than me. This person is more confident than Aisha."

74. Love or money?

Language / Skill practiced: Comparative adjectives
Time: 15 mins
Language level: Pre-intermediate to intermediate

Write, "Which is / are better…" on the board followed by prompts such as, "love / money," "the country / the city," "dogs / cats," "rice / bread," and "being intelligent / being beautiful." Divide the class into pairs. Each pair takes it in turns to ask "Which is / are better.." questions using comparative adjectives. For example:

Student 1: Which is better, love or money?
Student 2: I think love is better than money because it is more valuable. Money is easy to find if you work. Which

are better, dogs or cats?
Student 1: Dogs are much better. They are more faithful, more obedient. I hate cats. Which is better, rice or bread?
Student 2: Rice. It's more filling and easier to make!
Which are …..

And so on.

75. Blindfolded directions

Language / Skill practiced: Directions / Imperatives
Time: 20 mins
Language level: Elementary to pre-intermediate

Divide the class into two teams and ask them to stand at one end of the classroom. Each team nominates one student to stand at the other end of the room. Blindfold this student. Arrange a "maze" of tables and chairs between them and their team. Each team must now call out directions in order to direct their blindfolded teammate towards them. For example, "Turn left! No, left!! Ok, straight ahead." Every time they hit a chair or a table make them stop for 5 seconds. The team whose student arrives first, wins.

76. Map reading

Language / Skill practiced: Directions
Time: 15 mins
Language level: Elementary to intermediate

Draw a very simple street map on a piece of paper. Draw a landmark, such as a big hotel on this map. Create as many copies of this map as you have students in the class. In addition, create further copies of this map but with additional locations marked on it, such as a library, a swimming pool and so on.

Divide the class into pairs and ask them to sit back to back. Give one student from each pair, student A, a street map with just the one landmark. Give the other student, student B, a map with the additional locations marked. Student B must give student A directions from the initial landmark to all the other places on the map. Student B marks these places on the map. When student B's map is completed ask the students to compare maps to see how similar they are. Students can now swap roles and repeat the activity.

77. Animal clock

Language / Skill practiced: Telling the time
Time: 20 - 25 mins
Language level: Elementary to pre-intermediate

Draw a simple clock on the board, complete with the numbers one to 12. Next to number one write A/B, next to number two write C/D, and so on until number eleven, where you write U/V/W, and number 12, where you write X/Y/Z.
Write the word, "mouse" on the board and explain that the first letter of the word represents the hour hand and the last letter the minute hand. So M= 7 and E= 15: 7:15 or quarter past seven! Or, "Zebra" Z=12 and A=5: 12:05 or five past 12. Put the students into pairs to take it in turns saying animals and replying with the correct time.

78. Clock race

Language / Skill practiced: Telling the time
Time: 15 mins
Language level: Beginner to pre-intermediate

Draw 10 or so, simple clocks on the board, each set to a different time. This will only take you two minutes or so. Divide the class into two teams and ask each team to stand in a line as far away from the board as your classroom can manage. Call out a time. The first students in both of the two lines must run to the board and slap the appropriate time. The first student to do this wins one point for her team. These two students go to the back of their line and you call out a new time for the next 2 students.

79. My beautiful living room

Language / Skill practiced: Prepositions of place / Furniture
Time: 15 mins
Language level: Elementary to pre-intermediate

Ask each student in the class to draw a simple plan-drawing of their living room. Issue each student another sheet of blank paper and put them into pairs sitting back to back so they can't see their partners drawing. Each student takes it in turn to describe their living room while their partner draws according to their instructions. For example, "It's a big rectangular room. In the top left hand corner is the TV. The TV is on a small table. Next to the TV on the right is a big window…." (Be alert to students trying to peek a look at their partner's drawing!) After 10 minutes stop the activity and allow the students to compare their drawings.

80. It's my life

Language / Skill practiced: Various
Time: 15 mins
Language level: Elementary to pre-intermediate

Write the following words on the board: Likes, dislikes, family, holidays and favorite food. (Or, indeed, any other prompts you choose) Each student writes down five sentences about themselves on slips of paper using the words on the board as prompts. For Example, "I really like dancing but I don't like any sport. I have two brothers. I went to England on my last holiday. My favorite food is Korean food."

Collect the slips of paper and read them out one by one to the class. The class tries to guess who wrote which sentences.

81. Articles shout out

Language / Skill practiced: Articles
Time: 20 mins
Language level: Upper intermediate to advanced

Divide the class into teams of three or four. Prepare a text suitable to the level of your students but omit selected articles. Read out the text at a measured speed. Whenever a member of any team hears a sentence that should contain an article but doesn't, they should call out, "Article!" If they have called out correctly then award one point to their team, incorrectly minus one point. They gain a further point if they can insert the correct article. After you have finished reading the text and declared a winning team, give each student a copy and go through the text once more as a class identifying all the missing articles.

82. Cheater!

Language / Skill practiced: Cardinal numbers / Plurals
Time: 20 to 25 mins
Language level: Elementary to pre-intermediate

Divide the class into groups of three or four. Take out a pack of cards and check that all students can correctly identify all the cards. Next hand each group a pack of cards and ask one student to deal them out equally (or as equally as possible.) The object of the game is to get rid of all of your cards.

The player to the left of the dealer begins by laying any number of cards she chooses onto the middle of the table and claiming they are one, two, three or four aces. If any student in the group thinks she is lying he can say, "cheater" and the cards are turned over. If she was cheating then she must put the cards back in her hand. If not then the student who accused her of cheating must put the cards into his hand. It is the next students turn to lay down two's in the same way and say "one two," "two twos," "three twos" or four "twos." Again any of the other students may accuse him of cheating if they wish, the cards are turned over and returned to the student who laid them down or given to the accuser. The game continues with the next student laying down threes and so on. Of course the game can become very tense when there are lots of cards in the middle and no one wants to be the one to pick them all up!

83. Bing bong bang

Language / Skill practiced: Cardinal numbers
Time: 15 mins
Language level: Beginner to pre-intermediate

Arrange the class in a circle and ask the students to start counting in turn. For example:

Student 1: 1
Student 2: 2
Student 3: 3

And so on. Now tell the students that multiples of 3 are Bing and they must say, "Bing." So,

Student 1: 1
Student 2: 2
Student 3: Bing
Student 4: 4
Student 5: 5
Student 6: Bing

And so on. Now tell them that multiples of 4 are Bong and they must say, "Bong." Continue counting. Now tell them multiples of 5 or 6 are Bang, and they must say "Bang." Continue counting. Have a few practice rounds first and then start eliminating students from the game when they make a mistake. The last student to remain is the winner.

84. Ordinal bing bong bang

Language / Skill practiced: Ordinal numbers
Time: 15 mins
Language level: Pre-intermediate to upper-intermediate

As above, only replace cardinal numbers with ordinals e.g. "first, second, third" and so on. This makes it suitable for more advanced students.

85. Compound word quiz

Language / Skill practiced: Compound words
Time: 20-25 mins
Language level: Intermediate to advanced

Prepare a list of sets of compound words which each contain a common word. For example, "timetable," "overtime," "dinnertime" and "bedtime." Divide the class into teams and write the words "table," "bed," "over" and "dinner" on the board. Award one point to the first team to correctly guess the common word, "time." Continue for four more rounds with new words awarding a point for each correct guess. Now ask the groups to prepare their own list of sets of compound words which each contain a common word. Then invite one student from each group to come to the board and, as you did, write just part of the compound words on the board. The other groups attempt to guess the common word and get one point if they do so.

86. What did you buy?

Language / Skill practiced: Expressions of quantity
Time: 15 mins
Language level: Elementary to pre-intermediate

Arrange students into a circle. Start the activity with the sentence, "I went to the mall and I bought a bottle of water." The student to your left must repeat your sentence and add another expression of quantity and object to it, for example, "I went to the mall and I bought a bottle of water and a pound of pork" The student to her left repeats the sentence and adds another expression of quantity and object, for example, "I went to the mall and I bought a bottle of water, a pound of pork and two pairs of pants." And so on.

If you wish to add a competitive element to the game, eliminate students from the game if they forget an object or if they make a grammatical mistake.

87. Thank you so much!

Language / Skill practiced: Polite requests
Time: 45 mins to 1hr
Language level: Pre-intermediate to upper-intermediate

This activity takes a little while to set up. Initially you need to teach or revise polite requests. If you choose, you can do this by asking some of your students for items they have on them. For example, "Would you mind giving me your watch please, Alicia? Thank you," "Do you think you could pass me your book please, Mario? Thank you," "I wonder if you could give me your pencil please, Gabriel? Thank you." Students can now ask you for their things back using the polite requests that you modeled. Ensure that they also say thank you when they receive back their items.

Now bring out a set of playing cards and check that the students can correctly identify all the cards. Also elicit the words, "deal" and shuffle."
Students work in groups of four. The object of the game is to collect "sets" of four cards, for example, four aces, four tens, four kings and so on. No flushes or straights or what have you. When a student collects a set they are placed to the side and are equal to one point.

One student shuffles and deals the cards out equally to each student in her group. One student (the youngest or whoever you choose) begins by asking one of the other students, by name, for any card he would like to help him collect a "set." For example, "Antonio, would you mind passing me the eight of diamonds, please?" Antonio, if he has the card, MUST give it to the student who asked, who then says thank you. Because they received a card they can ask the same student or another student for another card. If Antonio, or whoever is asked for a card, doesn't have the eight of diamonds, or any other card he is asked for, then he simply says, "Sorry, I don't have it" and it is then his turn to ask someone for a card. The game starts slowly but students quickly become aware of who is looking for sevens or kings etc. and can work out who is likely to have what cards. When all the cards are gone add up who has the most "sets." This person is the winner. There's just one more very important rule which adds a lot of fun to the game. When a student receives a card but forgets to say, "thank you," which is very common, especially if she has just made a set and is excited, she must return the card and her turn ends.

88. Tongue twister demo

Language / Skill practiced: Pronunciation
Time: 15 mins
Language level: Elementary to upper intermediate

Give each student a tongue twister as homework e.g. "She sells sea shells on the sea shore" or some such. In the next class ask each student to come to the front of the class, write their tongue twister on the board, and demonstrate to the class how quickly they can say it. When everybody has had a go, students vote on who performed the best and, if you wish, who performed the worst!

89. General knowledge quiz

Language / Skill practiced: Various
Time: 20 to 30 mins
Language level: Pre-intermediate to upper-intermediate

Elicit the concept of General Knowledge from your class before conducting a short General Knowledge quiz using questions such as, "What nationality was Einstein?" "How many continents are there?" etc. There is no need to keep score at this point unless you wish. Now divide the class into groups of four or five to write their own General Knowledge quiz. You can, if you wish, ask them to divide their questions by category so they have two science questions, two sports questions and so on. It is also worth reminding the students that they must, 100% sure, know the answer to their questions as you may not! When each group has finished ask them to read their questions, in turn, to the class and award points to each group for correct answers.

90. Partial pictures

Language / Skill practiced: Modal verbs / Adverbs of possibility and probability
Time: 15 mins
Language level: Pre-intermediate to intermediate

The old school method of doing this relies on an OHP projector, but you can now, of course, use a computer and projector or even an interactive whiteboard. Project an image of a person, animal, building or whatever onto the whiteboard but almost completely cover it so that students can only see a small part of the image. Invite students to predict what the image is, using modal verbs and adverbs of possibility and probability. Gradually reveal more and more of the image while students continue to guess until the whole image is revealed. For example:

S1: It might be a tiger?
S2: It may be a painting.
(teacher reveals more)
S2: It could be a building, right?
S3: Maybe it's a tower.
(teacher reveals more)
S1: Is it a building? I mean, it's probably a building
(teacher reveals more)
S3: It must be a building. Is it the Empire State Building?
(teacher reveals more)
S1 It is. It's the Empire state building.
Teacher: Good, well done. A lot of good language there. Ok next one.

91. Four in a row tenses

Language / Skill practiced: Tenses appropriate to students' level
Time: 15 mins
Language level: Elementary to pre-intermediate

Draw a eight by eight, or bigger, grid on the board. In each cell write a word of your choosing, for example "Dogs," "Yesterday," "Coffee" and so on. Next to each word, write "P" for positive, "N" for negative or "Q" for question. Divide the class into two teams, A and B. Announce the tense you will use for the game, perhaps present perfect continuous. Ask team A to go first by picking one word from the grid and telling you a grammatically correct sentence in the present perfect continuous. This sentence must be either positive, negative or a question depending on the letter you have written next to the word. If they do this correctly, rub out the word and replace it with a red mark. It is now Team B's turn to pick a word and make a sentence. If they do this correctly rub out the word and replace it with a blue mark. The first team to get four colored marks in a row either horizontally, vertically or diagonally is the winner.

92. Tornado

Language / Skill practiced: Various
Time: 20 to 25 mins
Language level: Elementary to intermediate

Draw a 5 by 5 grid on the board and label the horizontal cells A to E and the vertical cells one to five. Each cell denotes a question, which only you know, scored 1 to 5 depending on the difficulty of the question. Questions for an elementary class, for example, might include, "What is the past tense of grow?" (2 points) "What is the opposite of interesting?" (3 points) And so on. In addition, three of the cells should be special, "Tornado" questions and three of the cells special, "Pass over" questions.

Divide the class into two teams, A and B. Invite team A to pick a cell, for example C3, tell them how many points the question is for and ask them the question. If they get the question right they, of course, get the points. It is now team B's turn to pick a cell and so on. When a team picks a "Tornado" question, however, if they get it wrong, they lose all the points they have gained. If a team picks a "Pass Over" question and answer incorrectly, then they give all of their points to the other team.

Continue until all questions have been answered and you can declare a winner.

93. Half conditionals

Language / Skill practiced: Conditional tenses
Time: 15 mins
Language level: Intermediate to Upper-Intermediate

Write, on slips of paper, sentences in several different conditional tenses. Cut these sentences into their two clauses so that every student in the class has one clause e.g. half a sentence. If you have an odd number of students then take a clause yourself too. So, for example, in a sentence such as, "If it rains today, I'll have to use my umbrella," one student would have, "If it rains today" and another, "I'll have to use my umbrella." Students stand up and read their clauses to each other until they find their partner clause. When every student has found their partner ask them to read out their sentence. As a class identify which conditional clause it is and its meaning.

94. Animal Antics

Language / Skill practiced: 2nd conditional
Time: 15 mins
Language level: Pre-intermediate to intermediate

Put students into pairs. Students take asking and answering questions beginning, "If you were a / an animal." For example:

S1: If you were a dog, what would you eat?
S2: I'd eat meat! If you were a tiger, where would you live?
S1: I'd live in India. If you were a giraffe, what other animals would you hate?
S2: I'd hate lions because they eat me. If you were a …..

And so on.

95. If this person were….

Language / Skill practiced: 2nd conditional
Time: 30 to 40 mins
Language level: Upper-intermediate to advanced

Write on the board the words, "Animal," "Color," "Car," "Food," "Drink," "Sport," "Plant," "Smell," "Weather" and "Country." Ask one student to leave the room. When this student has left, select another student in the classroom to be "the one." As a class decide which animal this student would be if he were an animal, which color he would be if he were a color and so on. Ask the student outside the classroom to return and invite her to ask questions of the class using the second conditional form and the prompts on the board. For example:

Teacher: Ok come in again Sofia, thank you.
Sofia: If this person were an animal, which animal would he or she be?
Member of class: This person would be a very dangerous tiger!
Sofia: Oh! Ok, If this person were a color, which color would he or she be?
Member of class: definitely black, really black
Sofia: Hmm, so someone dark and dangerous! What about car? What car would they be?

And so on. When the student has asked all her questions ask them to guess which student the class are referring to. Repeat with another student leaving the room.

96. Grammar swat

Language / Skill practiced: Various
Time: 20 mins
Language level: Elementary to intermediate

This is an excellent activity to help your students revise before tests. Prepare, on pieces of card, sentences in various structures. Stick these on the wall around the classroom. Divide the class into two teams and ask students to stand in the center of the room. Issue a flyswatter to a member of each team. Call out a clue to the teams, such as "A tense we use to talk about things we do again and again." The students with the flyswatters must, following advice from their team, run to the appropriate sentence and hit it with their flyswatter (in this case the sentence "I get up at 6:30 am.") The first team to do this successfully wins one point for their team. If they hit the wrong sentence, then they lose one point. Examples of other sentences you might use include:

"I must get up earlier": A sentence illustrating personal obligation.

"I'm going to watch the football tonight": A sentence illustrating future plans.

"That must be John at the door": A sentence illustrating near certainty.

"I've been to Italy": A sentence illustrating language to talk about experiences.

97. Problems, problems…

Language / Skill practiced: Advice
Time: 15 mins
Language level: Elementary to intermediate

Revise language for giving advice, such as "Why don't you..," "You should..," "You could…" and so on. Ask students to note down three problems they have. These can be silly e.g. "I'm too handsome" or real, e.g. "I'm having trouble getting here in time for the lesson." Divide the class into groups of three. Each student takes it in turn to tell her group one of her problems and the other students respond with advice. For example:

S1: I feel really tired today
S2: Oh dear, Why don't you have a cup of coffee.
S3: Yes, good idea. Or you could go outside in the break

to get some fresh air.
S1: Ok thank you.

When all groups have finished giving their problems and receiving advice, invite students to tell the class any particularly good pieces of advice they received.

98. Name ball

Language / Skill practiced: Names
Time: 10 mins
Language level: Elementary to advanced

This is a great warmer for the first day of class when students do not know each other's names. Bring a ball into class and arrange students in a circle. Say your name and throw the ball to another student. She says her name and throws the ball to another student and so on. After a few minutes, when the ball has come to you, throw the ball to another student and say his name. This student throws the ball to another student and says her name. After 5 minutes, stop the activity. Students should now have a good idea of their classmate's names.

99. Listen to me!

Language / Skill practiced: Language to show interest
Time: 15 mins
Language level: Pre-intermediate to advanced

The practice of language to show interest, such as "Uh huh," "Oh, really?" "Oh," "Did you?" "go on," "I see" etc. is often neglected in the ESL classroom but is a very important communication skill.

Divide the class into pairs and give each student a short text to read to their partner. Students take it in turn to read their texts to their partners who must attempt to sound as interested as possible. After two minutes, students swap partners and repeat the activity. Students keep swapping partners until they have read their text to five different people. Stop the activity and ask students to tell you who they thought the best listener was. Tell this student a short story so they can demonstrate their amazing listening skills to the class.

100. Map Race

Language / Skill practiced: Countries, nationalities and people
Time: 15 mins
Language level: Elementary to intermediate

Arrange the class in two teams, A and B facing the board. Call out a country. The person at the head of each line must run to the board and place their finger on the country. The first student to do so, wins 1 point for their team. They win a further point if they can then correctly pronounce the country name, another point for the nationality, and a final point if they can say what we call people from this country. For example, "The Philippines, Filipino, a Filipino / Filipina." So there are a total of four points to be won on each round. They then go to the back of their team's line and you call out a new country for the students at the head of the lines to race to.

Continue until every one has had at least one go and then declare a winner.

101. A good sentence?

Language / Skill practiced: Various / Error correction
Time: 20 to 25 mins
Language level: Elementary to upper-intermediate

Prepare a list of approximately 20 sentences that your students said in the previous lesson. Ensure that roughly half of them are grammatically correct. Divide the class into groups of three or four and give each group a copy of the sentences and five minutes to look them over. Call out the sentences at random and ask the groups if they are good or bad sentences. Award each group one point for a correct answer. After a bad sentence, invite the groups to correct the sentences and award a further two points to the first group to correctly call out the correct version.

102. Word sprint

Language / Skill practiced: Sentence structure
Time: 15 mins
Language level: Elementary

A good activity for younger students who need to burn of some energy.

Prepare three sets of slips of paper on which you have written vocabulary you wish to practice. So, each word is repeated three times; one set per team. Divide the class into three and have them sit on the floor in their groups. Give each student in each group a slip of paper. Assign each team a part of the white board, either left, right or center and give each team a whiteboard marker. Call out a word. The three students with this word written on their slip of paper stand up and run to their part of the whiteboard to write a sentence using this word. The first team to write a grammatically correct sentence wins one point for their team. Repeat until each student has had a go and all the words are gone.

Other books by this author

<u>102 ESL Games and Activities for Kids</u>

<u>Basic English Grammar: A Guide for New and Prospective ESL Teachers</u>

<u>English Grammar Exercises: A Complete Guide to English Tenses for ESL Students</u>

Made in the USA
Lexington, KY
04 January 2016